Smuggling in Devon

by
Frank Graham

Published: 1965
Reprinted: 1986

ISBN No. 0 907683 29 0

N. J. Clarke Publications
Tollgate Cottage
Tappers Knapp
Uplyme
Lyme Regis
Dorset

"SMUGGLERS"
Coloured soft ground etching by J. A. Atkinson, 1808.
By permission of the Trustees of the National Maritime Museum.

CONTENTS

	Page
Smuggling in Devon	5
North Devon	6
Cruel Coppinger	7
Lundy Island	8
Epitaphs and Churchyards	9
A Titled Smuggler	13
John Rattenbury	15
The Mutter Family	22
Smuggling Inns	26
Smuggling Methods	31
The Signal	35
The Preventive Service	39

Smuggling in Devon

Devon and Cornwall have always been important smuggling areas. The nature of their coasts, with numerous small harbours, their proximity to France and the Channel Islands, their remoteness from the control of the central authorities, have all contributed to foster the running of contraband, or free trade as its followers termed it. Smuggling stories in Cornwall are legion, and every harbour has some authentic history of the contraband trade. In Devon however smuggling incidents are less common and little true history can be discovered. The lack of information is not due to any lack of smuggling encounters but because less careful record has been kept of them. Cornishmen boasted of their smuggling exploits, the men of Devon kept them dark. Althought it was a Devon smuggler, John Rattenbury, who wrote the only real smuggling autobiography, it is noticeable how reticent he is about smuggling methods. After all his own son was still in the business, and Rattenbury only wrote his memoirs in retirement.

Smuggling in Devon started early and its first followers were fairly open in their work. They did not hide their activities; they simply defied authority. Neville Williams in his fine book – "Contraband Cargoes" – thus describes the Devon smugglers in the 16th century.

"The men of the West Country went their own sweet way. The seadogs of renown – circumnavigators, founders of colonies, leaders of maritime enterprise – looked on smuggling as part and parcel of their profession. It was the most natural thing in the world for Sir John Gilbert and Richard Hakluyt the elder to be involved in smuggling a load of valuable copper at Dartmouth in 1580; they were too proud to do it in a hole-and-corner way. They boasted they would interpret the law of the land to suit their own convenience as they did the law of the sea; and they were determined never to pay duties on their shares of prizes captured at sea. Small wonder that an investigation of the wine trade at Exeter in 1576 showed that of 275 tuns imported only 77 had paid duty. No one bothered about port officials trading on their own account, providing they did not interfere with the traditional ways of merchants. Christopher Blackoller, collector at Dartmouth and member of a prosperous Devonshire family, had his cellars full of prohibited goods. When Dartmouth was visited by the plague, the local vessels as a matter of course worked from Salcombe and Torquay, where there were no officials. Blackoller did not bother to send a deputy to take charge there, but hoped merchants might send him word of what they owed – in fees to himself as much as in duties to the Crown. It was a highly convenient arrangement. Long after the plague had gone, Dartmouth vessels were still crowding into Salcombe."

"There were high goings-on at Barnstaple in North Devon. Each year the Customs men co-operated with local merchants in shipping cargo after cargo of grain. The Earl of Bedford, the local magnate, was most upset when the Government took action against his tenants. He assured the Chancellor of the Exchequer that his town was 'very well governed, well given in religion and serviceable to the Queen'. He reminded the Chancellor that the country was desperately short of bullion – a fact painfully clear to the financial experts, who must have agreed with the Earl that the Barnstaple smugglers did an inestimable service in bringing home gold for the corn they had taken to Spain. Time and again reports reached Westminster of the malpractices of the 'lewd officers' in charge of the port; and eventually a large-scale enquiry was set afoot. The villain of the piece was Roger Norwood, the searcher. From very humble origins he had grown in six years to be a man of substance and 'purchased land daily'. With the customer as his partner in crime he bought up all the corn he could lay his hands on, and stored it in a large barn on the cliffs by Hartland Point, ready for loading into ships that anchored outside Barnstaple bar. And they did very well out of bribes. A Tavistock merchant was amazed to see stacks of leather being loaded from the quay at night and called the customer. 'Here it is, blind knave', he pointed; but the customer laughed in his face. Another merchant came to the conclusion that nothing but prohibited wares passed in and out of Barnstaple. Any local men who refused to co-operate with the officers had informations lodged against them. To guard against similar treatment from their opponents, Norwood and his confederates hired a stooge who would inform against every cargo in which they had interest 'before any other can do so', and then automatically withdraw the charge. After the enquiry, the customer and searcher complained to Burghley that the commission for discovering their misdemeanours had been maliciously procured. With great fairness the Lord Treasurer asked for a further report by fresh commissioners. They reached identical conclusions."

North Devon

For geographical reasons North Devon was not so important for smuggling as the south coast. The journey round Cornwall was dangerous and considerably lengthened the voyage. The direct route from the southern ports to France and the Channel Islands was therefore favoured.

Near Lynmouth is the beautiful cove of Lee Bay. Above the bay runs the road to the moorland hamlet of Martinhoe. It passes along the cliff edges nearly all the way. At one point the road approaches within a few yards of the precipice. Here is a chasm known as the Smuggler's Leap.

"Many years ago", we are told, "when dealings in contraband paid better than such dealings today, a smuggler rode fast over these cliffs pursued by a King's officer. The exciseman had the better nag of the two, and drew rapidly on his quarry. As pursuer and pursued came abreast of the chasm they rode neck and neck, and the latter swerved aside to avoid the officer's grasp. The movement was too much for the horse, who, with a wild snort, went over the brink. But the smuggler did not fall alone. Feeling himself going, he clutched wildly at his enemy, and they rolled into the abyss together. It is said that when their bodies were discovered by the seaweed gatherers they were locked together in a vice-like grip which had hurled them into eternity."

There are a number of caves in this area associated with smuggling. John Page describes one of their storehouses near Lee Bay whose entrance was so narrow that a few bushes carefully arranged could hide it. Near Ilfracombe, Brandy Cove and Samson's Bay (Samson was a local smuggler) recall smuggling days.

Cruel Coppinger

However the most famous North Devon smuggler was "Cruel Coppinger" who combined the trade with wrecking also. We have already described the legends woven around his name by the Reverend Hawker in our booklet on Cornish smugglers. About the real Coppinger little is known. His name was Daniel Herbert Copinger or Coppinger and he was wrecked at Welcombe Mouth on December 23rd 1792. He was given shelter by a yeoman farmer called Arthur, the event being commemorated by an inscription on a window-pane which was preserved for many years.

> "*D. H. Coppinger, shipwrecked December 23rd, 1792;
> kindly received by Mr. Wm. Arthur.*"

Next year he married Ann Hamlyn and the marriage is recorded in the registers of Hartland Church.

"For about two years he carried on his nefarious business of smuggling, and stories are still told of the various methods he adopted of outwitting the gauger. His chief cave was in the cliff at Sandhole, but another is pointed out in Henstridge Wood, a couple of miles inland. On one occasion, perhaps after Coppinger's time, the caves were watched so closely that the kegs of brandy which had been landed were deposited at the bottom of the *zess*, as the pile of sheaves in a barn is called, of an accommodating farmer. The gauger, who had his suspicions, wished to search the zess, but the farmer was so willing to help him in turning over the sheaves that his suspicions were allayed, and he went away without finding any of the incriminating articles. On another occasion the result was not so satisfactory for the farmer. On the arrival of the gauger, he produced some empty kegs in order to give his wife an opportunity of hiding a supply of valuable silks which had been left in their care. The safest place she could think of in her hurry was the oven, but she forgot that it had been heated for baking a batch of bread. The result was that, although the gauger failed to find them, they were burnt to ashes."

Little else is known of Coppinger. He became bankrupt in 1802 and was imprisoned in the King's Bench. On release he lived for many years at Barnstaple, and, although he had separated from his wife, he received an allowance from her.

Lundy Island

Immediately beneath Marisco Castle, on Lundy Island off the north Devon coast, is a large cave in the cliff. The cave is about 10 feet wide, 10 feet high, and 40 feet long. The entrance is low and was originally hidden by a wooden hut. It is called Benson's Cave. Thomas Benson was a well-to-do Bideford merchant, once M.P. for Barnstaple, and known to have been engaged in smuggling in a big way. The cave was constructed by him to hide contraband. He was at the time the tenant of Lundy. Among his business activities was a contract to transport convicts to America. Instead he used them as slave labourers on Lundy; probably the cave is their handiwork. He was heavily fined for his smuggling activities and his estate near Bideford estreated in default of payment.

His final crime was to insure a vessel's cargo, secretly to take the cargo off the vessel, scuttle her, and claim the insurance money. The plot failed. The captain of the vessel was hung but the chief culprit, Benson, escaped by fleeing the country.

Near Ilfracombe is Chambercombe Old Manor House, a well known house of mystery. "In the year 1865, the owner chanced to notice a bricked-up window and, since he was puzzled to think of a room to correspond with it, he began to investigate with a pickaxe. He discovered a narrow, low-ceilinged room containing a handsome carved bed, on which lay the skeleton of a woman. It is believed that the remains were those of a Spanish woman who had been captured off a wreck by smugglers and had died on their hands. The room had a double floor, so that it is probable that the space between was used for smuggled goods." Squiers – Secret Hiding Places.

Epitaphs and Churchyards

In our book on Cornish Smuggling we quoted some epitaphs on Smugglers. For Devon we have only found tombstones in memory of excisemen. In the old church of Seaton, South Devon, can be seen a tablet recording the sad fate of William Henry Paulson, midshipman of H.M.S. Queen Charlotte, and eight seamen "who perished in a gale of wind off Sidmouth whilst crossing in a galley for the prevention of smuggling in the year 1817".

In the "weird, eerie churchyard of Branscombe, in which astonishing epitaphs of all kinds abound, is a variant upon the smuggler's violent end in the inscription to John Hurley's memory" which reads as follows:-

"Here lieth the Body of Mr. John Hurley, Custom House Officer of this Parish. As He was endeavouring to extinguish some Fire made between Beer and Seaton as a Signal to a Smuggling Boat then off at Sea He fell by some means or other from the Top of the Cliff to the Bottom by which He was unfortunately Killed. This unhappy Accident happened the 5th Day of August in the Year of our Lord 1755. Aetatis suae 45. He was an active and Diligent Officer and very inoffensive in his life and Conversation."

Churchyards were however not only used to bury the victims of smuggling but were a favourite rendezvous of the freetraders when alive. Many a vaulted tomb has been used by smugglers for hiding their contraband while churches and especially church towers and belfries were frequently used, often with the connivance of the parson or sexton. In the 18th and 19th centuries two of the vicars of East Budleigh were well known for their dealings with smugglers. It is perhaps natural since almost all their parishioners were engaged in the trade. The vicarage became the smugglers' headquarters, and an ideal place it was with rambling passages, hidden alcoves, and secret rooms. The vicarage was built in the fifteenth century and still stands although now a private residence. On one of the windows the smuggling parsons inscribed their names with a diamond. The pane can still be seen with the inscription:-

BRANSCOMBE CHURCH 1825

Matt Mundy Vicr.
Sept 24
1741
A. A. Stapleton Vicar
1794.

Writing of churchyards reminds us of the famous Brixham smuggler who was nicknamed "Resurrection Bob" and had as his headquarters a cave in the limestone cliffs of Berry Head. His real name was Bob Elliott and his band of smugglers caused the coastguards endless trouble. J. Page in his book called "The Coasts of Devon and Lundy Island" tells the following story which an informant heard from the lips of Bob's grandson.

"One week, when Bob was laid up with the gout, his crew arrived with half a dozen kegs of brandy for which they had been unable to find room in the cavern. So the kegs were concealed in Bob's cottage. But somehow the coastguard got wind of what had happened, and the cottage was visited. But Bob was dead. He had died during the night, it was said, and the officer out of respect withdrew his men without making any search at all. The coffin – a very large one, someone remarked, but then Bob was a big man – was duly brought, and soon a mournful procession left the cottage. But

> 'Twas his spirit they bore,
> Whilst, to keep from a roar,
> In a kerchief Bob buried his nose.

That night three coastguards met a coffin on the Totnes Road, accompanied by one who bore a strange resemblance to the buried Bob. To the eyes of the terrified officers this phantom glared.

> Like one whom they'd rather not name
> Whilst the nag cocked his tail
> Like a harpooned whale,
> And snorted a crimson flame.

Panic-stricken the men fled, and brought the tale to their commander. But that gentleman was no fool, and, keeping his own counsel, paid a nocturnal visit to the dead man's cottage. Here, under the shadow of the wall, amid roars of laughter, he heard Master Bob tell the story of his ruse. To the dismay of the smugglers, the officer walked in upon them, but, beyond giving them a sound rating, let them off scot free. Perhaps he was unwilling to make public how easily the King's men had been duped. But ever after the hero of the adventure was known as "Resurrection Bob."

Baring-Gould tells how in his own parish an old church-house was demolished. "The church-house was originally the place where the parishioners from a distance, in a country district, put up between the morning and afternoon services on the Sunday, and was used for "church ales". It was always a long building of two storeys; that below served for the men, that above for the women, and each had its great fireplace. Here they ate and chattered between services and here were served with ale by the sexton or clerk. In a great many cases these church-houses have been converted into taverns. Now this one had never been thus altered. When it was pulled down, it was found that the floor of large slate slabs in the lower room was undermined with hollows like graves, only of much larger dimensions – and these had served for the concealment of smuggled spirits. The clerk had, in fact, dug them out, and did a little trade on Sundays with selling contraband liquor from these stores".

"FOR OUR PARSON."

A Titled Smuggler

Not only was the parson often the friend of the smuggler but the landed gentry also played a part as financiers of the expeditions, as well as using their houses and estates for hiding their goods. And if the smuggler was arrested and brought before the Justices he often found a co-partner on the bench. This was the reason why it was often difficult to get a smuggler convicted in his own locality.

"The story is told of a certain baronet near Dartmouth, now deceased, who had a handsome house and park near the coast. The preventive men had long suspected that Sir Thomas had done more than wink at the proceedings of the receivers of smuggled goods. His park dipped in graceful undulations to the sea and to a lovely creek in which was his boathouse. But they never had been able to establish the fact that he favoured the smugglers, and allowed them to use his grounds and outbuildings.

"However, at last, one night a party of men with kegs on their shoulders were seen stealing through the park towards the mansion. They were observed also leaving without the kegs. Accordingly, next morning the officer in command called, together with several underlings. He apologised to the baronet for any inconvenience his visit might occasion – he was quite sure that Sir Thomas was ignorant of the use made of his park, his landing-place, even his house – but there was evidence that 'run' goods had been brought to the mansion the preceding night, and it was but the duty of the officer to point this out to Sir Thomas, and ask him to permit a search – which would be conducted with all the delicacy possible. The baronet, an exceedingly urbane man, promptly expressed his readiness to allow house, cellar, attic – every part of his house, and every outbuilding – unreservedly to be searched. He produced his keys. The cellar was, of course, the place where wine and spirits were most likely to be found – let that be explored first. He had a

SMUGGLERS HIDING GOODS IN A TOMB.

cellar-book, which he produced, and he would be glad if the officer would compare what he found below with his entries in the book. The search was made with some zest, for the Government officers had long looked on Sir Thomas with mistrust; and yet were somewhat disarmed by the frankness with which he met them. They ransacked the mansion from garret to cellar, and every part of the outbuildings, and found nothing. They had omitted to look into the family coach, which was full of rum kegs, so full that to prevent the springs being broken or showing that the carriage was laden, the axle-trees were 'trigged up' below with blocks of wood."

John Rattenbury

The most famous Devon smuggler was without doubt John Rattenbury of Beer, popularly known as the "Rob Roy of the West". His renown rests on his remarkable smuggling career, but his interesting and detailed autobiography has also contributed to his importance. We need not believe that he himself wrote the "elegant" English in which his life story is composed, but who the ghost writer was we haven't the slightest clue. The book is undoubtedly a reasonably true record of his smuggling career, taken down from his own lips, although many incidents are narrated in such a way as to put Rattenbury's point of view, which was not always the strict truth. An incident illustrating this point is the unsuccessful voyage of the Lyme Packet. Here E. Keble Chatterton (in his book King's Cutters and Smugglers, 1912) tells the story:-

"As one looks through the gaol-books and other smuggling records, one finds that there was a kind of hereditary custom that this running of contraband goods should pass on from father to son for generations. Thus there are constant repetitions, in different ages, of men bearing the same surname engaged in smuggling and becoming wonderfully notorious in this art. Among such family names must be mentioned that of Rattenbury. The man of whom we are about to speak was flourishing during the second decade of the nineteenth century, and his christian name was John. In November 1820 – it is significant how often this dark month crops up in the history of smuggling, when the weather was not likely to tempt those Revenue cruisers' commanders, who preferred the snug shelter of some creek or harbour – John Rattenbury happened to find himself at Weymouth. Into that port also came a vessel named the Lyme Packet, which was accustomed to trade between Lyme and Guernsey. But on this occasion the ship had just received the misfortune of carrying away her bowsprit – possibly in the Portland Race – and her master, John Cawley, decided to run into Weymouth for repairs.

"Whilst these were being taken in hand what should be more natural than that the Lyme Packet's master should drift into a local public-house ? Having brought up comfortably in that haven of rest, he was promptly discovered by his old friend Rattenbury, who had also made for the same house of refreshment. The usual greetings took place, and Rattenbury inquired how it was that Cawley came to be there, and an explanation of the accident followed. According to the skipper's own version, they got into conversation, and, over a glass of grog, Rattenbury volunteered the remark that if Cawley would be willing to sail across to Cherbourg to fetch a cargo of spirits he would pay him at a rate that would make it much more profitable than trading between Lyme and Guernsey. In fact he was willing to pay Cawley as much as twelve shillings a cask, adding that in one voyage this skipper, who happened also to be owner, would make more money thereby than in the regular course of trade in a twelvemonth.

"Such a proposition was more than a tempting one, and Cawley gave the matter his attention. Unable to resist the idea, he acquiesced, it being agreed that Rattenbury should accompany him to France, where they would take in a cargo of spirits, Cawley to be paid his twelve shillings for every cask they were able to bring across. So, as soon as the bowsprit was repaired and set in its place, the Lyme Packet cast off her warps and ran out of Weymouth harbour. She made direct for Cherbourg, where they anchored in the roadstead. Rattenbury now went ashore and returned accompanied by 227 casks of spirits made up in half-ankers. These were put on board and the voyage back to England commenced, the intention being to make for West Bay and land the goods somewhere near Sidmouth. Having arrived off the Devonshire coast, Rattenbury took the Lyme Packets boat and rowed himself ashore, landing at Beer Head, his object being to get assistance from the men of Sidmouth for landing his goods. It was then about 1 a.m. The captain of the Lyme Packet kept his ship standing off and on during the night, and hovered about that part of the coast till daybreak. But as Rattenbury had not returned by the time the daylight had come back, Cawley became more than a little nervous and feared lest he might be detected. Before very long – the exact time was 6.30 a.m. – Robert Aleward, a mariner on the Revenue cutter, Scourge, on turning his eye into a certain direction not more than three miles away, espied this Lyme Packet, informed his commander, and a chase was promptly begun. Cawley, too, saw that the Lyme Packet had been observed, and began to make preparations accordingly.

"He let draw his sheets, got the Lyme Packet to foot it as fast as she could, and as the three intervening miles became shorter and shorter he busied himself by throwing his casks of spirits overboard as quickly as he and his crew knew how. The distant sail he had noticed in the early morning had all too truly turned out to be the Revenue cutter, but he hoped yet to escape or at any rate to be found with nothing contraband on board. It was no good, however, for the cruiser soon came up, and as fast as the Lyme Packet had dropped over the half-ankers, so quickly did the Scourge's men pick

REVENUE CUTTER C 1800

The long bowstrip is characteristic of Revenue Cutters. An extended bowstrip allowed more sail and therefore greater speed. The fitting of such a bowstrip to any vessel other than a "Revenue Cutter" or "man of war" was illegal.

EXMOUTH C. 1840

them up again in the cutter's boats. Having come up alongside, the cutter's commander, Captain M'Lean, went on board, seized Cawley and his ship as prisoners, and eventually took both into Exmouth.

"Judicial proceedings followed with a verdict for the King, so that what with a broken bowsprit and the loss of time, cargo, ship, and liberty the voyage had in nowise been profitable to Cawley."

Rattenbury's account is very different. The blame for the loss is put on Captain Cawley, who, Rattenbury claims, was drunk during the critical periods of the trip and he is very bitter because the Captain turned King's evidence and revealed Rattenbury's connections with the attempt to run the contraband cargo.

He also very carefully hides from us the time when he actually worked for a short period for the Revenue authorities. In 1829 he served for a few weeks on the Tartar cutter. He mentions this fact in his Memoirs but he does not tell us the nature of the Tartar's commission, "and it is left for us to discover that the bold smuggler had taken service at last with the revenue and customs authorities, and for a time placed his knowledge of the ins and outs of smuggling at the command of those whose duty it was to defeat the free-traders. It was perhaps the discovery that the work of spying and betraying was irksome, or perhaps the ready threats of his old associates, that caused him to relinquish the work".

Rattenbury was born in 1778, the son of a village cobbler of Beer in South Devon. Before he was born his father had already disappeared, taken on board a man of war, probably by the press gang. His mother, however, was tough and self-reliant and brought him up "without receiving the least assistance from the parish, or any of her friends".

Young Rattenbury started his sea career at the early age of nine, fishing with his uncle, but quickly dropped the family connection when he lost the boat's rudder and was thrashed for his negligence. He was next apprenticed to a Brixham fisherman but found the life dull and after a few years he went privateering. But Rattenbury's career as a privateer was dogged with misfortune. Every voyage ended in catastrophe and eventually he gave up the life for good and settled down to smuggling, where he was more successful! Not that everything was plain sailing. Many a run with contraband failed and Rattenbury often found himself in gaol or on his Majesty's ships, but his ability to escape was remarkable, and the profits in smuggling were great. The successful voyages paid for the failures.

Page 19. Old Print. "SMUGGLERS ATTACKED". From a mezzotint after Sir Francis Bourgeois.

Page 21. Old Print. "SMUGGLERS DEFEATED". Also by Sir Francis Bourgeois. *By courtesy of the British Museum.*

One of his escapes took place at the famous Cornish hostelry called the Indian Queen. Rattenbury had been caught in an open boat in the Channel, tried at Falmouth and committed to Bodmin Gaol along with one of his companions. They travelled in two post-chaises, in company with two constables. "As our guards", he writes "stopped at almost every public-house we came to, towards evening they became pretty merry. When we came to the Indian Queen (a public-house a few miles from Bodmin), while the constables were taking their potations, I bribed the drivers not to interfere. Having finished, the constables ordered us again into the chaise, but we refused. A scuffle ensued. One of them collared me, some blows were exchanged, and he fired a pistol, the ball of which went off close by my head. My companion in the mean time was engaged in encountering the other constable, and he called upon the drivers to aid and assist, but they said it was their duty to attend to the horses. We soon got the upper-hand of our opponents." They then escaped across the moors and, meeting with another party of smugglers, they were assisted in their return to Beer.

The Mutter Family

One of John Rattenbury's associates was Abraham Mutter, a turf-cutter and wood merchant. He entered the smuggling profession in a curious way. The story is told in an article published in the Western Times and Gazette on May 11th, 1956.

"Abraham Mutter cut his turf and hewed his wood on the high land near Peak Hill, Sidmouth – the place is still known as Mutter's Moor – and sold them in Exmouth, Sidmouth and even in Exeter. For transport he had a few carts and a team of donkeys, and working these in shifts he hawked his wares over a very wide area.

"Excellent !", said Rattenbury to his colleagues, "Where better to hide our kegs than under a load of turf bound for some gentleman's house ?" – the gentry were great buyers of contraband – and the proposal was put to the industrious Abraham.

He agreed, and from then onwards made a great deal on the side by co-operating to the full with the smugglers.

Rattenbury was at the peak of his career at about this time and Mutter worked with him for several years, so profitably, it appears, that when Rattenbury eventually retired, Sam Mutter, who was a life long sailor, stepped into his shoes and continued to provide the supplies for his enterprising brother, and later for John, who had also joined the business.

Sam was evidently a determined character. He was caught several times by the Revenue men, and he served his time in jail. After one of these terms his friends waited outside the prison gates to celebrate his freedom, but were disappointed; he failed to turn up.

Three months elapsed – then he came in from the sea, with another load of brandy. He had various ways of bringing it in, concealing it under a load of cider apples and so on, and he followed the common practice of hiding it in lobster pots, to be picked up later by the fishermen.

At length, though, the coming of the railway killed this thriving industry, as it killed so many others. Trains pushing always westwards began to affect the turf and wood business, for on the one hand the men found it more profitable to work with steel than with donkeys and, on the other, coal steadily ousted the ancient turf. John Mutter slowly went out of business, and with his going one at least of the smugglers' lifelines was cut.

This, and the growing efficiency of the Revenue men, finally put an end to the trade that had proved so lucrative for so many years and to so many adventurers on the coast, men of Branscombe, Beer, and Sidmouth particularly."

In his "History of Salcombe Regis" J. Y. Anderson Morshead records the following statement from an old smuggler, one Henry Northcote, who mentions both Rattenbury and Mutter. "I have carried scores of kegs up the cliffs," he stated. "We used to strike a match and hold it in our hands a moment to call the boats in. The loads were then shouldered into a pit with a lid in Paccombe bottom, or by the turnpike on the hedge there, and waggoned on afterwards. Once they were in Slade cellar but the King (i.e. Revenue officers) called and they were only just started in time down the drain; it made the rats squeak. It was a pity for they were a nice lot of tubs. Two Branscombe farmers, Bray and Fry, were the main stays of the business. The goods used to come in a cutter called Primrose. She was owned in Portland and had been a gentleman's yacht. It was her J. Rattenbury steered with his foot, while he kept the French crew from lowering sail, when the King fired at him. She was taken often by the Coastguard, but generally had her papers right. She used to bring potatoes from Guernsey, but one day they caught her in a gale without ballast; she had just started her cargo and that determined them. They sawed her in half, for they said nothing else would stop her. I knew Rattenbury and have heard he cut the Officer up for crab bait, but he always laughed if it was thrown up at him, and said it happened down Dawlish way by a Sussex man. The last cargo was Mutter's laid up under High Peak. G. Walter watched all day from a furze bush but about 4 p.m. a stranger (gentleman to look at) came under Cliff and strolled right up to the tubs. The man in charge got as mad as fire, but he had to lump it for if he'd spoken they'd have taken him. The gentleman was smoking a cigar but they said he was armed secretly".

The sexton of Salcombe Regis also made a statement in which he told that "the main smuggler was Mutter of Harcombe who kept a public at Exmouth and when riding officers wanted to know if a run was on, they would go to his house for a pint, and if the old man could not show up it was look out for the next tide. He was more artful than Rattenbury. Two Branscombe farmers smuggled too. Dimond's brother kept Trow turnpike and informed against a a waggon that went through with goods. A procession was made through the three parishes with his likeness and then burned. Williams and Bray (the two farmer smugglers) paid for this."

Salcombe was an important smuggling centre. Kebble Chatterton records the following successful arrest of a smuggler in this area.

"Towards the end of June in the year 1818 William Webber, one of the Riding officers, received information that some spirits had been successfully run ashore at the mouth of this harbour, 'a place', remarked a legal luminary of that time, 'which is very often made the spot for landing' this class of goods."

Webber obtained the help of a private in the 15th Regiment, and learning that the goods had not yet been taken inland, decided to try and surprise those appointed to transport the tubs. In the evening they went to the spot and hid behind a hedge. They heard some men talking. One of them, James Trotter, remarked "We couldn't have had a better time for smuggling if we had lain abed and prayed for it."

"We can readily appreciate Thomas's ecstasy when we remark that it had now become rather dark and a sea-haze was beginning to spread itself around. For some time longer the two men continued to remain in their hiding-place, and then heard that Thomas and his accomplice had become joined by a number of other people. The sound of horses' hoofs being led down to the beach was also distinctly heard, and there were many signs of accelerated activity

SIDMOUTH IN 1836

going on. Presently there came upon the ears of the Riding officers the noise which proceeds from the rattling of casks, and from some convenient hiding-place, where they had remained, these were at last brought forth, slings were prepared, and then the load was placed on the backs of the several horses."

At this point the Riding Officer stepped forth. The smugglers were away like a flash. Only Thomas was caught. He was too busy arguing with his men whom he thought had been drinking from the casks which were "slack", that is not up to full weight.

Few of the smugglers' haunts near Beer and Sidmouth survive. The ancient tower of Salcombe church was a regular hiding place for contraband. About a mile from Beer is the fine Tudor mansion of Bovey House. During the latter part of the eighteenth century the house was empty and was much frequented by the free-traders, who were guarded by the ghosts which haunted the house and the lanes leading to it. Ghosts were always friendly towards smugglers and the places they used were often conveniently haunted by them.

Near the pretty village of Branscombe, a notorious place for smugglers, once stood "The Clergy House". It was pulled down near the end of last century because it was considered dangerous and insecure. It was a Tudor building and many strange stories were told about its former occupants and its secret hiding places. So many were these hidden chambers that the people of Branscombe used to say there was another house beneath the foundations. Many were the casks of brandy hidden in those vaults and many a smuggler must have taken refuge there.

Smuggling Inns

There are scores of inns in Devon and Cornwall which claim smuggling associations. Many of them even use the title of Smuggler in their name. Few however are genuine, and fewer still can provide real proof of their smuggling activities. In our booklets on Cornish Smugglers and Cornish Inns we have only been able to record half a dozen genuine smuggling inns of which only four survive today. In Devon we can only mention two since the site of Rattenbury's inn at Beer is unknown. The first is the Mount Pleasant Inn at Dawlish Warren which was unfortunately partly destroyed by a fire in 1955 but rebuilt on the same lines as before. Here is Charles Harper's story of smuggling at Dawlish Warren from his classic book "The Smugglers".

"The estuary of the Exe, between Exmouth and Starcross, was for many years greatly favoured by smugglers, for, as may readily be perceived to this day, there lay in the two-miles-broad channel, where sea and river mingle, a wide, wild stretch of sand, almost awash at high water, heaped up in towans overgrown with tussocks of coarse, sour grasses, or sinking into hollows full of brackish

SALCOMBE CHURCH 1825

THE SMUGGLER

water: pleasant in daytime, but a dangerous place at night. Here, in this islanded waste, there were no roads nor tracks at all, and few were those who ever came to disturb the curlews or the seabirds that nested, unafraid. In these twentieth-century times of ours the Warren – for such is the name of this curiously amphibious place – has become a place of picnic parties on summer afternoons, largely by favour of the Great Western Railway having provided, midway between the stations of Starcross and Dawlish, a little platform called the "Warren Halt". But in those times before railways, when the Warren was not easily come at, the smugglers found it a highly convenient place for their business. Beside it, under the lee of Langsten Point, there is a sheltered strand, and, at such times when it was considered quite safe, the sturdy free-traders quietly ran their boats ashore here, on the yellow sands, and conveyed their contents to the "Mount Pleasant" inn, which is an unassuming – and was in those times a still more unassuming – house, perched picturesquely on the crest of a red sand-stone bluff which rises inland, sheer from the marshy meadows. It was a very convenient receiving-house and signal-station for all of this trade, for it owned caverns hollowed out of the red sandstone in places inaccessible to the authorities, and from its isloated height, overlooking the flats, could easily communicate encouragement or warning to friends anxiously riding at anchor out at sea. The lights that flashed on dark and tempestuous nights from its high-hung rustic balcony were significant. The only man who could have told much of the smugglers' secrets here was the unfortunate Lieutenant Palk, who lay wait one such night upon the Warren. But dead men tell no tales; and that ill-starred officer was found in the morning, drowned, face downwards, in a shallow pool, whether by accident or design there was nothing to show. As already remarked, the Warren was a dangerous place to wander in after dark.

"It is quite vain nowadays to seek for the smugglers' caves at Mount Pleasant. They were long ago filled up.

"In these times the holiday-maker searching for shells is the only feature of the sands that fringe the seaward edge of the Warren. It is a fruitful hunting-ground for such, especially after rough weather. But the day following a storm was, in those times, the opportunity of the local revenue men, who, forming a strong party, were used to take boat and pull down here and thoroughly search the foreshore; for at such times any spirit-tubs that might have been sunk out at sea and carefully buoyed by the smugglers, awaiting a favourable time for landing, were apt to break loose and drift in-shore. There was always, at such times, a sporting chance of a good haul. But, on the other hand, some of the many tubs that had been sunk months before, and lost, would on these occasions come to hand, and they were worth just nothing at all, long immersion in salt water having spoiled their contents, with the result that what had been right good hollands or cognac had become a peculiarly ill-savoured liquid, which smelt to heaven when it was broached. The revenue people called this abominable stuff, which, as Shakespeare might say, had 'suffered a sea-change into something new and strange' by the appropriate name of 'stinkibus'."

The second smugglers' inn is on Burgh Island. The Pilchard Inn was once the haunt of pirates. It is situated at the foot of Burgh Island, a ten-acre paradise in the centre of Bigbury Bay, approximately 400 yards off shore. The Pilchard Inn bears on its sign the date 1395, the pirate device of the skull and cross-bones, with the legend "Mors Vincet" (Death Wins). Inside the inn was preserved – until recently – a unique pirate flag grey and crumbling with age. It is reputed to have belonged to Tom Crocker, Prince of Smugglers, and part-time pirate, who had his base here in Elizabethan times. A modern inn on the mainland has been named after him. In the inn parlour is a big fire-place and at the side is a rough carving of Tom Crocker and opposite is the face of an Excise Man, or so legend says, since they have been sadly mutilated. There is a cave in the vicinity called "Tom Crocker's Hole" and here tradition says his loot was hidden.

The Pilchard Inn, Burgh Island

Smuggling Methods

In Devon in the 18th century the smuggling boats coming from Roscoff in Britanny landed their cargoes directly on to the beach or in the harbour. They had little to fear from the authorities. They were met by large numbers of people, some of whom were armed with cudgels or blunderbusses. The men armed with cudgels received the name of Batmen. Their job was to see that no one interfered with the operation. The cargoes were landed quickly and the smugglers made off as expeditiously as they could. The men on shore then had the job of dispersing the contraband and taking it inland. This was done on the backs of ponies and men. The men were usually paid 1/- a night and 5/- bonus if the run was successful. Those who carried the tubs over their shoulders were called Tub Men. The harness they wore and the flat tubs were specially designed for easy transport. The smugglers were generally too strong to be interfered with while at work, and one of the precautions they took was to make villagers face the wall when the smuggling cavalcade passed through a hamlet. Then if a smuggler was later arrested the country folk could truthfully say that they had seen nothing.

"Them that ask no questions isn't told a lie, watch the wall, my darling, while the gentlemen go by."

The vagaries of the law helped the smugglers. Until the 19th century, although it was an offence to bring contraband ashore, it was no offence to sell smuggled goods. Hence the taverns could advertise Genuine Crow Link. This was schnapps which had been smuggled through Crow Link near Beachy Head.

After the close of the war with France, in 1815, and particularly when coastguards became more efficient after 1831, the old fashioned "runs" became impossible and greater care had to be taken. The practice of sinking cargoes off the coast in selected spots became almost universal. The smugglers would come in to land after dark and drop their cargo overboard, anchored a certain distance below the surface, for the local men to lift when the coast was clear. Always two or three alternative spots were chosen before the smugglers set out. The land parties included "Flashers" to signal that the coast was clear. Sometimes the pan of an old flint-lock pistol was used to give the necessary flash. But this primitive method, which could be seen by the excisemen also, was replaced by a special lantern with a long funnel which could direct its light in a given direction. By day the smuggling craft signalled by pre-arranged handling of sails.

The coastguards were given prize-money if cargoes were captured and they were regularly out in their boats "creeping" with grapnels of all shapes and sizes over likely spots. Many of them were, however, bribed. As one writer expressed it, "they wore fog spectacles with bank-note shades."

Various methods used to 'raft' wine or spirits to keep them hidden from the coastguards on patrol.

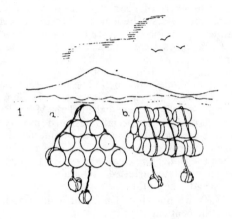

Many kegs would be tied firmly together and weighted down to float under the surface.

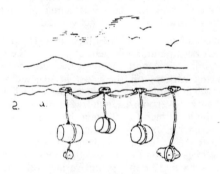

A floating line of kegs suspended under the water which would be carried by the sea or river current to a point where the look-outs would be waiting.

NOTE.—The sinking-stones are bent on, and kept on deck till just before slipping.

As the preventive services improved in efficiency the smuggling boats began to hide some of their cargo. False bulkheads and decks were regularly used. The ship's water-tank, carefully doctored, was a favourite hiding place.

The actual financing of smuggling and the profits made are something of a mystery. That big capital was involved is fairly obvious and it was generally held among smugglers that if they could save one cargo out of three they were well recompensed for their work. Commander Shore in his book "Smuggling Days and Smuggling Ways" reveals the following "trade secrets" which were confidentially divulged to him by an old smuggler. The information is extremely interesting. We therefore present it here in full. It refers only to the trade in spirits, probably in the West Country.

"If I intended bringing over a cargo, I would arrange for all the likely parties I knew of to meet me on a certain day for the purpose of deciding on the number of tubs. Each person would 'venture' so many, paying down to me, on the spot, £1 for each tub ventured. Another £1 per tub would be lodged in the bank to pay expenses. Supposing we arranged for a hundred and fifty tubs, I would take the £150 advanced, look out for a likely boat, and make a bargain with the owner for the trip across. If the captain preferred it he would be paid a lump sum, say £100, out of which he paid the crew, arranging with them as best he could – there were always plenty of chaps ready to chance a run across in those days, and then, you see, they could always venture a few tubs themselves, if they liked.

AN OLD-TIME SMUGGLER

"Sometimes the freighter would pay down half the amount agreed on before starting, say £50, besides which he would agree for £25 per man of the crew, of which £20 would be paid down. If times were bad, of course men could be got for less, £15 or £10 maybe. The captain would then engage a crew on his own terms, paying, perhaps, £3 or £5 per man down.

"In buying the tubs over in France, £1 would fetch twenty-one shillings, while the tubs would cost generally 18s. each, according to the bargain you made with the merchant, who, in addition, always allowed one tub in a score, and two in a hundred, which was called 'scorage' tubs, and always went to the owner of the boat, who, before sharing profits, would deduct so much for 'freight and average.'

"Sometimes the tubs could be bought for as low as 16s. each, the difference going into the pocket of the purchaser, to cover small expenses, such as 'sinking-stones,' food, etc., for the crew.

"A tub – or half-anker, as it used to be called before my time – weighed about fifty-six pounds when full, and contained four gallons of brandy, costing from four to five shillings per gallon in France; the same costing in England thirty-six shillings, duty paid. So, by getting the stuff 'run' clear of duty – thirty-two shillings a gallon it was in those days – a pretty good profit could be made on a cargo of a hundred tubs.

"Each tub cost the venturers £2, the same, if charged duty, costing about £6.

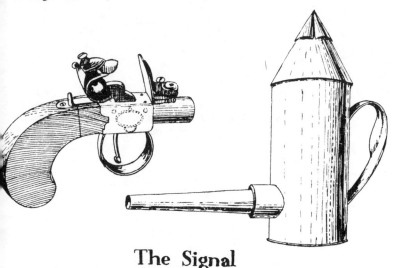

The Signal

Speed was essential in moving smuggled goods from the beach to the 'safe' storage areas. The illustration shows a quick and convenient way of carrying kegs over the shoulders of porters who were known in the trade as 'flaskers'.

"Of course, if the cargo was lost, the venturers just lost the £1 paid down, the other pound being only paid to the freighter after the tubs had been delivered, and if they were lost the money was drawn out of the bank again and paid back to the venturers.

"The tubs were always supplied by the merchant ready 'slung'. I generally bought my cargoes at Roscoff, though I have been to Cherbourg and other ports for goods. The spirit you got in those days was beautiful stuff – mild, and fine-flavoured; indeed, you can't get anything like it now.

"The spirit was almost always supplied uncoloured – white brandy it was called – a tub of colouring mixture being supplied with the tubs by the merchant for the purpose of colouring the spirit after it had been run. I sometimes made my own colouring mixture with burnt sugar, and it was just as good as that supplied by the merchant.

"The average strength of the liquor supplied was 70° above proof, but I have known cargoes brought over as much as 180° above proof. You see, it could be brought over at less expense like that, a hundred tubs making three hundred when mixed to the right strength; besides, brandy of this strength was sold cheaper in proportion, or at about thirty shillings the four-gallon tub. Of course it required fewer tubs and caused less trouble to the merchant. But if cheaper to buy – costing to the venturer, when reduced to its proper strength, about 2s. 6d. a gallon – the mixing gave a lot of trouble. It had to be done after landing, and oftentimes there was a difficulty in getting enough tubs to put the liquor into after it was mixed, so that, on the whole, it gave more trouble than it was worth, in my mind."

An East Indiaman would bring supplies of tea, silks and spices from the East.

COASTGUARD IN 1830 UNIFORM

The Preventive Service

For convenience the history of smuggling can be divided into two periods. First there is the "free trade" period. During this time measures for prevention were so poor that the smuggler almost carried on his trade with impunity. The eighteenth century and early nineteenth were the halcyon days of the freetrader. Second is the scientific period which commenced with the end of the wars with France in 1816. During the "free trade" period the smuggler was not however left entirely alone. There was a preventive service which was however weak in manpower and often corrupt. On shore there were the officers of the Customs and Excise and afloat there were the Revenue cutters. The Revenue officers quite often called in the help of soldiers to assist them in their work. In the year 1784 the following cruisers were employed in the Customs Service in Devon and Cornwall. The figure in brackets denotes the number of the crew.

Plymouth	—	Ranger (21)
Plymouth	—	Wasp (20)
Exeter	—	Alarm (26)
Dartmouth	—	Spider (28)
Looe	—	Squirrel (20)
Falmouth	—	Hawke (18)
Falmouth	—	Lark (20)
Penryn	—	Lurcher (30)
Scilly	—	Tamer (25)
St. Ives	—	Brilliant (30)
St. Ives	—	Dolphin (26)

The Revenue ships were however often inefficient, stayed in harbour during bad weather, sometimes indulged in smuggling on their own, and were no real threat to the smugglers who had fine boats, were superb seamen, and were prepared to fight when necessary.

"The shifts and expedients of the Commissioners of Customs for the suppression of smuggling were many and ingenious, and none was more calculated to perform the maximum of service to the Revenue with the minimum of cost than the commissioning of privateers, authorised to search for, to chase, and to capture if possible, any smuggling craft. 'Minimum of cost' is indeed not the right expression for use here, for the costs and risks to the customs establishment were nil. It should be said here that, although the Acts of Parliament directed against smuggling were of the utmost stringency, they were not always applied with all the severity possible to be used; and, on the other hand, customs officers and the commanders of revenue cutters were well advised to guard against any excess of zeal in carrying out their instructions. To chase and capture

RIDING OFFICER AND DRAGOONS

a vessel that every one knew perfectly well to be a smuggler, and then to find no contraband aboard, because, as a matter of fact, it had been carefully sunk at some point where it could easily be recovered at leisure, was not only not the way to promotion as a zealous officer; but was, on the contrary, in the absence of proof that contraband had been carried, a certain way to official disfavour.'
The happy idea of licensing private adventurers to build and equip vessels to make private war upon smuggling craft, and to capture them and their cargoes, was an extension of the original plan of issuing letters of marque to owners of vessels for the purpose of inflicting loss upon an enemy's commerce; but persons intending to engage upon this private warfare against smuggling had, in the first instance, to give security to the Commissioners of a diligence in the cause thus undertaken, and to enter into business details respecting the cargoes captured. It was, however, not infrequently found, in practice, that these privateers very often took to smuggling on their own account, and that, under the protective cloak of their ostensible affairs, they did a very excellent business; while, to complete this picture of failure, those privateers that really did keep to their licensed trade generally contrived to lose money and to land their owners into bankruptcy."—C. HARPER.

The size of the trade, the complete disregard for the law which characterised the smugglers, and the heavy losses to the Revenue finally forced the government to act.

They decided to establish a coast blockade. Starting with Kent and Sussex they established blockade stations manned by naval men who were stationed in the Martello towers along the coast. Where towers were not available barracks were built. Here we have the beginning of the modern coastguard station. Gradually the system was extended, although in a modified form to cover all smuggling areas. An important part of the new service were the Riding Officers who had been in existence for over a century. However, in the past they had not been numerous enough and by themselves had been easily overawed. They had therefore depended upon the help of the military. "It was not a happy idea this of setting dragoons to catch smugglers – rather indeed like setting elephants to catch eels."

The Coastal Blockade was detested by the civil population and not popular with the navy. It was difficult to obtain volunteers. We are told that "in consequence of the small number of men-of-war's men who could be induced to enter the force, the roll was thus filled, for the most part – if by blue-jackets, by 'waisters' (the least intelligent of a ship's crew), or, which was more frequent, by unskilled, though hardy, Irish landsmen, whose estrangement from the sentiments, habits and religion of those placed under their surveillance seemed to point them out as peculiarly adapted for a service whose basis consisted in an insidious watchfulness over others, and a hostile segregation from their fellow-men."

The system of discipline in the service was harsh and brutal. It was a "continual flog – flog – flog." A letter written to the Sussex Advertiser in 1821 speaks of "deeds fit for the barbarous countries of Africa only in their savage state, men being driven like slaves to their duty with the cat at their backs, and for the least deviation from the straight line of duty are thrown into the hold, ironed, and kept there until the pleasure of their Commander be known."

Public feeling against the system was very strong and in the year 1831 the Coast Blockade was abolished. It was replaced by a "Preventive Water-Guard" later altered to coastguard. It was made up of volunteers, not pressed men.

"The early coastguardmen had a great deal of popular feeling to contend with. Officers and men alike found the greatest difficulty in obtaining lodgings. No one would let houses or rooms to the men whose business it was to prevent smuggling, and thus incidentally to take away the excellent livelihood the fisherfolk and longshoremen were earning. Thus, the earliest stations of the coastguard were formed chiefly out of old hulks and other vessels condemned for sea-going purposes, but quite sound, and indeed, often peculiarly comfortable as residences, moored permanently in sheltered creeks, or hauled up, high and dry, on beaches that afforded the best of outlooks upon the sea."

The Revenue Coastguard, which was established in 1831, was transferred from the control of the Board of Customs to the Admiralty in 1856.

Smuggling however is still not finished, although the methods may have altered. Only recently two men were convicted at Teignmouth and sentenced to prison for smuggling whisky and cigarettes. The Urban Council now uses a picture of a smuggler with a cask on his back in all their publicity for the resort, because, as their publicity officer states, "in the minds of the nation Teignmouth is a smuggling town."